NATURE'S SECRECY

COLLECTED POEMS

AMIYO BASU

Copyright © 2017 by Amiyo Basu

All rights reserved

Thank you for buying an authorized edition of this book and for complying with the copyright laws by not reproducing, scanning, or distributing any part of it in any form without permission.

ISBN 978-1-54460-274-5

To my family

"Painting is poetry that is seen rather than felt, and poetry is painting that is felt rather than seen."

— Leonardo da Vinci

CONTENTS

Nature's Secrecy	1
Hello Tinkerers	2
Take Your Time	4
Leonardo	6
Amsterdam A Lovely City	9
Fluidic Air	10
About the Music and the Mind	11
The Fifth Graders	12
Late Summer Rain	14
A Sonnet	15
Mobile	16
The Red Bird in My Memory	18
Yesterdays and Tomorrows	19
A Windowless School Cafeteria	20
Listen Closely so You Can Hear	22
Seemingly Motionless	23
Saying Isn't Enough	24
Road Markers	25
Melodic Tune	26
A Brief Meeting	27
The Written Words	28
In the Midst	30

Charlie's World	31
Chasing that Little Ball	33
While You Sleep	34
ABOUT THE AUTHOR	35
ACKNOWLEDGMENTS	36

Nature's Secrecy

It was all a secret.
Only the morning sun,
the cool breeze,
the fluttering leaves,
and the blooming flowers
had a hint.

And they quietly passed on
the secret to the blowing wind
that carried over and whispered
to a distant anguished soul.

The soul let it be known
to the nearby foothills
and to the dew drops
on a blade of grass.

And, the nature's secret
was out for all to admire and
absorb.

Hello Tinkerers

Keep on inventing the *wheel* and let
others figure out how to stop it
from rolling downhill.

Did the inventor of the pen
fret about using the pen
to nick someone? Would we
then have a pen to create the
best of literatures?

And, to today's tinkerers, your
device may cause inconveniences
or damage. But, don't let that stop you
from dreaming the impossible.

We the humans are supposed to
create new things which, if
misused, can be destructive
—think of a hammer.

The message to the makers

of new things: invent the latest

wheel and move on to your next

creation.

We'll figure out how best to use it.

Take Your Time

Look around – clocks are
everywhere. The wall clock,
the desk clock, the grandfather
clock (who came up with that
name!), winding and clock
with glowing digits.

Don't forget the watches. The
pocket watch graduated to the
wrist watch and some have jewels
on them.

The daily routine is thoroughly
driven and controlled by time.
Yes, we need to know the time
for our need not to be dictated
by the two hands (if you worry
about ticking of the second hand,
it's hopeless).

Did the cave painters at Chauvet, France
need to finish their paintings on a certain
day, or did they simply take their time

creating the remarkable

imagery that lasted over 20,000 years?

I'd like to think they painted those

durable art at their leisure.

Yet I need to finish this poem on

time. It'd be just wonderful if someone

years from now might ponder if this writer

had a deadline to meet.

Leonardo

Not just in Mona Lisa, Leonardo saw beauty in a piece of uncut stone just as in a human face, and reverentially made them alive.

Observing how a flowing stream could cut through solid rock, Leonardo devised ways to derive power as he saw the grandeur in a body of water as it splashed and sparkled.

No one before him sketched human musculature at its deepest tissue, the beating of a heart, the curvature of bones, the workings of the brain with the delicate touch of an artist.

Leonardo drew people, and their gods, sculptured stones to immortalize the splendor of human physique. He sensed passion in listless objects and took pains to give them dynamism.

Leonardo marveled at all creations with
oddity and profound wonder. He wanted
to know how a bird took to air, and the how
horse raced at a gallop. He purchased
caged birds and set those free!

He exemplified parachutes and flying
machines hundreds of years before they
came to be. He gazed into the cosmos,
and understood why was the sky blue.

Leonardo created art through science,
and made science artistically pleasing
to the senses.

Salutare Leonardo da Vinci!!

The two poems given in page 9 can be read individually as 'Amsterdam' and 'A Lovely City' or together as a single poem as 'Amsterdam, A Lovely City.'

Amsterdam

The vacation home was
A four-story house;
In this quiet neighborhood,
Smiling faces greeted the newcomers,
And despite the daily grind
The traffic wasn't rushed.
Along with the street performers
With an international flavor
The countryside was lovely,
Among gorgeous surroundings.
And Van Gogh and Rembrandt
And their paintings spoke to all;

A Lovely City

In a nice part of Amsterdam
In a not-so-busy street,
We spent a week of summer.
Cars and bicycles shared the road.
The rush was rather smooth.
The city plaza had street vendors
From all different continents;
And cosmopolitan in nature.
With nice, charming people
Anne Frank's house stood bold,
Museums represented humanity,
In this lovely city.

Fluidic Air

Air, the liquid we can't see;
move your hands, feet, and
as you turn the liquid air will
move with you.

The wave of this liquid will carry
you onward, and will flow with
and around you.

Even when you leave, the air
will remember and reveal that
you were there.

And your fleeting presence
will be reminisced.

About the Music and the Mind

Origami, folding a paper once, twice,
a few more times, and soon a paper crane appears.
Or it could be a paper animal or a butterfly!

Nature unfurls a leaf like magic, a flower
blooms with artistic beauty and elegance, or beans
sprout and grow into vibrant plants.

The musical scales, too, have folds among octaves
that become a memorable score or a song
lifting the spirit.

Even the human brain begins with folded layers
which develop by ushering wondrous
possibilities in all its splendor.

Does the human mind offer similar latency-
staying folded but may not reach its full potential
unless it's carefully cultivated?

Then why not unfold our minds, so they can touch
and inspire all beings as one entity and make them
aware and fulfilled?

The Fifth Graders

How'd I go about explaining to the fifth graders

the physics behind a vehicle as it moves from rest?

It was not something I could or should do—so I thought.

But like so many other things that one ends up doing,

there I was in front of thirty or so young minds

talking about force, inertia and all that.

Could I make those fresh faces interested,

would the physics mean anything to them?

would they grasp the concept—I wondered!

The time came to build models to show

what those theories meant. Those young bright

gleaming eyes understood enough to stay engaged.

I was mesmerized and watched with fascination how

those little hands picked up the various pieces and put

together the models with a kind of ease, in a rather

matter of fact way.

Might this be poetry in creating objects

that moved, rolled, and pitched? How simply they

took to the task, how easy they made it feel!

There I stood among those curious minds that beamed

so much confidence and boldness, which gave me

a sense of pure joy mixed with tender certainty.

Late Summer Rain

The rain came early that morning;
it was a torrent! At summer's end,
and the beginning of fall,
I looked forward to a cool, crisp
morning in early fall, not rain.

But, that late summer rain was
somewhat special. When the rain
stopped, a double rainbow appeared
covering the horizon end-to-end.

The crisp cool weather returned
the next day and like magic
rejuvenated the meadows
with bright yellow flowers that
sparkled for days, keeping the winter
at bay, at least for the time being.

Winter, now you need to wait your turn!

A Sonnet

And then she came

Like a breath of fresh air

As if everyone knew her name

And she belonged there.

She sparkled as she moved

In her flowing pink attire

Her lively energy grooved

With grace without mire.

She set apart the scene

Wherever she went

The charm of her being

And the dimply dent.

Soon she fell asleep in her mother's lap

Since the one-year-old was ready for her nap.

Mobile

For me, the word mobile has been
more than something that moves
(or a phone to some).

In my mind, a mobile and the movement
of his little hands or feet made are
linked forever.

The bright eyes, the babble, the cooing
were delightful. The wonderment began
the moment he arrived on this earth.

That day became the first day of many days
to come, and that feeling of fulfilment grew
over days and months and years.

And the feeling of that first day would be
everyday till the rest of my days.

Those babbling that I heard over the music of that mobile I attached to his crib would be an unending source of joy and happiness.

The Red Bird in My Memory

The winter was over, and the bare trees

outside my window was in quiet contemplation;

kind of had a naked beauty as a painter might say.

The leaves began to appear around March

and by April the greenbelt kept the promise

of its namesake.

Along came the red bird, a Cardinal, that morning

glistening its bright red feathers on a tree branch

among all that greenery and the shrubs.

Other birds were around too, I'm sure. But on

that April morning that Cardinal was my bird

of choice. Soon the Cardinal flew away

to catch a worm or to get a berry.

But would my memory of that morning

keep the Cardinal on the branch or

let it fly away so it could get its meal of choice?

Yesterdays and Tomorrows

It seemed just yesterday, the schooling
was done, got the degrees the
university had to offer, then came work,
learning, career, and the family.

Jobs took me to cold, warm, and
in between places in big and small
towns with usual excitements,
adjustment, and challenges.

There were successes and some failures,
happiness and gloomy days for things
that matters, or at times they didn't!

And, rather unexpectedly, a day came
notifying that I have more yesterdays
than tomorrows.

A Windowless School Cafeteria

A rural small-town school
with a few hundred students
was rather quaint. The cafeteria
was the gathering place for the
students for their meals, parent-
teacher meetings, and the rest.

At the school suggestion box, an
anonymous note was left that the
cafeteria had no windows and this
needed to change. The student
newspaper took notice, wrote a
small article, but the news didn't
catch on.

A loner of a student named Perry
who would sit at the back of his class
had just a couple of friends. Perry
liked to eat alone and kept to himself.
His family farm had a barn with no windows.
He remembered how his grandpa put a
light shaft using his wartime submarine
days' experience.

Perry, in his ingenious way, modified

that idea and shared with his buddies.

On a play night at the school when everyone

was busy, Perry and his buddies went up to

the roof, put a pipe through a small hole

and fixed two mirrors in the pipe, one at

the roof and the other inside the cafeteria.

The fixture ran down by a water pipe and

was hard to find unless one looked for it.

The next day at lunch time, a shaft of bright

light flooded the cafeteria. The principal

wasn't amused and Perry was called to his office.

Fearing the worst Perry showed up in

his office and the principal was about to

discipline him. There was a commotion

outside his office so he stepped out.

Perry's entire class showed up to support

Perry. At the next parent-teacher meeting,

it was voted that the cafeteria would be called

Perry's scope.

Listen Closely so You Can Hear

Listen, and hear your footsteps
in a forest among the sounds of
the gentle wind, the falling leaves
and the nearby falling water.

Now here comes a plane subsuming
the noise of nature. And the mouse
that was trying to survive the impending
attack from the owl, became deaf to the
oncoming threat and lost the fight.

Be quiet, make less noise if you
can and let the nature keep its
sounds.

Seemingly Motionless

The home planet earth

spins around its axis fast,

traverses its orbit encircling

the sun even faster.

The planets and the stars within

the galaxy Milky whirls among

cluster of galaxies and are moving

away from each at incredible speed.

The science says dark matter is

holding these bodies together.

The gently swaying tree branch

outside my window seems quite

content and in peace.

Saying Isn't Enough

In a world full of people,

you hear people say—

"we want to save the world."

Then there are some,

they live by their deeds,

not words.

These deeds become

legends for their

selfless acts, hard work,

and sacrifice.

It's not saying, but doing.

And, that holds the key to

saving the world.

Road Markers

On that bright sunny day, the
naturally landscaped
highway looked as green as ever.

The black tar stretched and
crisscrossed the long northern
US-Canada border.

The travelers were reminded
where they were as the mile
post changed to kilometers.

The Romans built roads with
milestones which still exist
around Rome.

If these miles, kilometer
markers last a thousand years,
would the historians be confused?

Surely, the markers would get
the last laugh!

Melodic Tune

It was a bird that chirped

to wake his flock, gather

and go on a flight.

The squirrel heard the chirping,

mimicking the birds, passing it to the

trees, branches and the leaves.

The wind carried the sound

over the meadows,

up and over the mountain

and down to the shores.

The waves caught the harmony,

danced to it that became the

tune that the fish sang.

The lives in the water

brought the melodic tune

back onto the land.

And the tune became the

melody for all to sing and dance.

A Brief Meeting

Boarding a flight for yet another meeting
seemed quite tedious at the Calcutta airport
that Summer afternoon. Couldn't help but notice
the nuns in their blue-bordered saris sitting nearby
with tears flowing down their cheeks.

The nuns lived their lives serving
others, lessening suffering and misery.
Then what might have caused them to
be so sick at heart—I pondered!

The answer came from another nun
dressed in a similar attire who stood near me.
I approached her, the revered
Mother (now Saint) Theresa, with my question.
She gently took my clasped hands in the palm
of her hands, showering her blessings.

She answered, her sisters were bidding
her goodbye as she was leaving on
trip. I realized what it meant for the sisters to part
with her, who forsook her life for the humanity and
personified divinity amid utter despair.

The Written Words

The words, the thoughts, the meter, the rhymes
that you crafted, drafted, reflected, replicated,
wrote and rewrote at your desk, or at a café, had
the power beyond you and your spheres.

You let your imagination flow onto a paper or a
computer screen. You wrote what came to mind
at the first instance, followed by your memorable
moments showing your flashes of brightness.

You told the world what it didn't know, couldn't know,
or even knew that it had a need to know and
enriched the minds of many with surprises, suspense,
or tragic situations.

You portrayed your dreams as if those were real and your real
life as dreams, and made your dreams your life and the lives
as dreamy. You didn't stop writing when nothing made sense
and in the process you broke the rules and made new ones.

You found meaning in things, and then changed the meanings with word by word, phrase by phrase. You penned the last chapter as the first and first as the last and made the middle appear and disappear at will.

Your adventurous journey with words brought smiles or tears, angered, or pleased all who read or just glanced at your work. And you passed on your making to the readers and made the writings indelible.

In the Midst

You could be in a crowded city,

at a pristine beach, or in a

moonlit night in a desolate desert.

You observed the faces, saw the waves

lapping at your feet, or witnessed the

mesmerizing reflections of the sand.

Someone, somewhere may read and think

how a crowd be so energizing,

a beach so enticing, or even the

nightly desert sands so mystifying?

Search among those kind faces, in the

luminous waves, or the glistening sand,

and the mystery will be revealed that you

absorbed in your own self.

Charlie's World

In a group of islands, in the middle of the ocean
Charlie grew up in a modest home.
His growing up was ordinary, attending a privileged
school made possible by a benevolent donor.

His classmates became future presidents, business
leaders. Average student that he was, Charlie joined
the Army. His Army buddies called him Pineapples,
the core product of his home islands.

Then came an attack on a Sunday morning
to the airbase not far from Charlie's home.
The islands became the source of war.

The life beyond the Army took him to a
big city, and his sort of a regal look landed
him an acting role. But his approaching
middle age and the Polynesian demeanor
weren't in his favor.

His return to the islands brought him
back to his roots, and Charlie came face to face
with events occurring generations ago

as these islands were taken over by traders
and growers.

He realized the treaty signed with the then
island monarch didn't include transfer of the
title of the land to the locals. The miles and miles
of pineapple plantations brought laborers from
other places.

Charlie's life came full circle. He was
back at the ocean, riding the waves and
wistfully reminiscing what could have been,
but was not to be.

Chasing that Little Ball

Couldn't that ball be a little bigger,

or the stick (someone named it a club)

be a little fatter?

Can't even see the hole where the ball

has to go. Is it over the horizon or

into a neighboring city?

Boy, does it take time, not seconds or minutes,

but hours (which can seem like days)

to finish the game?

Then there are hazards affectionately

called traps or bunkers. Did I just see

someone break his club in two?

And, if the play goes well, the satisfaction

is momentary indeed, because the pain

restarts at the next game all over again.

While You Sleep

Eons ago, in that land seers

put their profound knowledge

into action of introspection.

Those thoughts were

put in words by successive

peers which were then written

down that transcended time,

generations, civilizations, wars

and destruction, and those writings

are eternal. Why eternal? They say,

if you want to know you, look within

and all around, and you too will begin

to know the *you* which is awake

even when you are in deep sleep.

ABOUT THE AUTHOR

Amiyo Basu, Ph.D. is a retired mechanical engineer, whose career spanning four decades, involved researching and developing new and advanced technologies. By nature and training, he is an innovator and holds numerous patents and publications.

These collected poems are reflections of Dr. Basu's interpretation of his surroundings. They are a blend of cheerful and thoughtful musings showcasing his perspective on the world.

Dr. Basu lives near Austin, Texas with his wife so they can be near their son and his family.

ACKNOWLEDGEMENT

I would like to express my gratitude to my family, friends, and to those who provided support and inspiration. Many thanks to my wife for assisting with the cover design and saw me through this book. Special thanks to my son, his wife and my many good friends at the Baca Writing Club for proofreading, and offering valuable suggestions.

Some of these poems will appear in the upcoming Round Rock Rambling publication.